DAZZLING DIGGERS

Tony Mitton and
Ant Parker

KINGFISHER
LONDON & NEW YORK

Diggers are noisy, strong, and big.

DAZZLING DIGGERS

For Kate, Tim, Henry, and Angus—T. M.

KINGFISHER
LONDON & NEW YORK

Text copyright © Tony Mitton 1997
Illustrations copyright © Ant Parker 1997
Cover design by Peter Clayman 2014
Published in the United States by Kingfisher,
120 Broadway, New York, NY 10271
Kingfisher is an imprint of Macmillan Children's Books, London.

Distributed in the U.S. and Canada by Macmillan, 120 Broadway, New York, NY 10271
EU representative: Macmillan Publishers Ireland Ltd, 1st Floor, The Liffey Trust Centre,
117-126 Sheriff Street Upper, Dublin 1, D01 YC43.

LIBRARY OF CONGRESS CATALOGING-IN-PUBLICATION DATA
Mitton, Tony.
Dazzling diggers/Tony Mitton (author) : Ant Parker
(illustrator). — 1st American ed.
p. cm.
Summary: Animals operate digging machines that scoop, lift, move
rubble, squish through mud, and help buildings tower up tall.
[1. Excavating machinery—Fiction. 2. Animals—Fiction.
3. Stories in rhyme.] I. Parker, Ant. ill. II. Title.
PZ8.3.M685Daz   1997
[E]—dc21   97-9944   CIP AC

ISBN: 978-0-7534-5304-9

Kingfisher books are available for special promotions and premiums. For details contact:
Special Markets Department, Macmillan, 120 Broadway, New York, NY 10271.

For more information, please visit
www.kingfisherbooks.com

Printed in China
20 19 18 17 16

FSC
www.fsc.org

MIX
Paper from
responsible sources
FSC® C116313

Diggers can carry and push and dig.

Diggers have shovels to scoop and lift,

blades that bulldoze, shunt, and shift.

Diggers have buckets to gouge out ground,

breakers that crack and smash and pound.

Diggers move rubble and rocks and soil,

so diggers need drinks of diesel oil.

Some have tires and some have tracks.

Some keep steady with legs called jacks.

Tires and tracks grip hard as they travel,

squish through mud, and grind through gravel.

Diggers go scrunch and squelch and slosh.

Splish
Splash
Splosh

This dirty digger needs a really good wash.

Diggers can bash and crash and break,

make things crumble, shiver, and shake.

Diggers can heave and hoist and haul.

Diggers help buildings tower up tall.

Drivers park neatly, down on the site.

And then they all go home. Good night!

Digger parts

levers

these control different parts of the digger

tire

this helps the wheel grip the ground and get the digger moving

bucket

this is for digging and scooping out

jack

this holds the digger steady when it is lifting or digging

piston

this is a strong pump that makes parts of the digger move around

breaker

this is for cracking concrete or lumps of rock

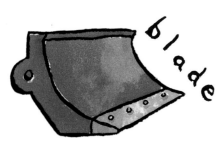

blade

this is for knocking down and pushing along

tracks

these help the digger travel over slippery or bumpy ground